BASKETBALL GAME

At first Allen made no attempt to be too friendly with the girl next door. After all, she was white, and he would have plenty of opportunity to be with girls of his own color when he went to school in the fall. But Rebecca wasn't so inhibited. He interested her, and why was it impossible for them to spend time together?

So it started; an innocent walk along the street was reported back to Rebecca's father and after that she would only come across and practice basketball with him when her parents were out of the house. And he was warned off her. 'The white folks around here at the college have been looking at you sitting out there with that white girl. And they don't like it, son,' his own father told him. 'You just be careful. Don't get in a position where anyone can even think you might've been doing something wrong with her, You understand?'

Nashville, Tennessee, might not be as bad as Alabama or Mississippi, but still prejudice destroyed the tentative relationship growing between Allen and Rebecca, because he was black and she was white.

Julius Lester was born in St Louis, Missouri, in 1939. He took a B.A. in English at Fisk University, and has been both a photographer and a singer-songwriter, an instructor in Black History in New York, and has hosted a weekly radio programme. He has also recorded two albums of original and Afro-American songs. He is married, has two children and lives in New York.

Other books by Julius Lester

LONG JOURNEY HOME
TO BE A SLAVE

BASKETBALL GAME

Julius Lester

PUFFIN BOOKS

Puffin Books, Penguin Books Ltd, Harmondsworth, Middlesex, England
Viking Penguin Inc., 40 West 23rd Street, New York, New York 10010, U.S.A.
Penguin Books Australia Ltd, Ringwood, Victoria, Australia
Penguin Books Canada Limited, 2801 John Street, Markham, Ontario, Canada L3R 1B4
Penguin Books (N.Z.) Ltd, 182–190 Wairau Road, Auckland 10, New Zealand

—

First published in the U.S.A. 1972
Published in Great Britain by Kestrel Books 1974
Published in Peacock Books 1977
Reissued in Puffin Books 1982
Reprinted 1983, 1985, 1986

—

Made and printed in Great Britain by
Richard Clay (The Chaucer Press) Ltd,
Bungay, Suffolk
Set in Monotype Garamond

TO MY EDITOR, PHYLLIS FOGELMAN,
THE UNSUNG HEROINE

ONE

I

ALLEN hadn't wanted to move to Nashville, Tennessee. His father, though, had told him it would be all right. 'The Lord works in mysterious ways and you don't question the workings of the Lord.' But preachers always said something like that when they didn't know what else to say.

Allen was glad, however, that his father hadn't been sent to a church in Alabama or Mississippi or even Arkansas, where both his parents were from. Down there colored people really had it hard and he had spent more summers than he wanted to remember at his grandmother's house outside Pine Bluff, Arkansas. At least Nashville was a big city and not a little country town like Pine Bluff and, as far as southern cities went, it was supposed to be a pretty good one. It was segregated, of course, but so was every place except New York and Chicago.

Allen didn't mind segregation. Kansas City, Kansas, where he'd spent his fourteen years until that summer of 1956, was segregated too, but unlike Pine Bluff, there weren't signs everywhere jabbing you in the eye. He hated to go down-town in Pine Bluff because of the signs – COLORED and WHITE – in stores, at the bus and train stations, on the buses, and everywhere else they could nail them. His parents, however, never went into any place where they had to walk underneath a COLORED sign to get in.

There hadn't been many signs in Kansas City. Everybody knew where they could and couldn't go. So the signs weren't really needed. He presumed everybody in Pine Bluff knew also. But the signs were there nonetheless. In the few days he'd been in Nashville, he hadn't seen many signs, but he knew that there was no place downtown he could go and sit down and eat a hamburger. He could get one to take out, but his parents wouldn't let him. 'If they don't want you to sit down at the counter like everybody else and eat, then you don't want to give them your money,' his father told him. Allen supposed that that was right, but sometimes he got awfully hungry when they went shopping and wished his parents hadn't had such strong principles.

He'd never been able to understand why white people hated Negroes, or why his father hated them in return. In Allen's world, whites were ghostly shadows whom he saw through the window of the car but had no real contact with. A few years ago he hadn't even been exactly sure what white people looked like and asked his third-grade teacher. The class had laughed at him and he supposed now that it had been a dumb question, but unlike the others, his father didn't work for white people and his mother didn't work at all. Rev. Anderson would have sooner seen his wife dead and in the grave than to see her working in some white man's house, the only job she could have gotten. When the laughter had quieted, the teacher told him, 'Well, the way to tell a white person is to look at their noses. All white people have big noses.' For a while that had been his only guide, and he found it to be a fairly accurate one. White people sure did have some noses on them. Like snouts. Eventually, however, he learned that there was an easier way to identify them. They didn't have any color and their hair was different. But it wasn't that easy, either, because his mother didn't have much color and her hair was straight. And he would've sworn his grandmother was white if she hadn't been his grandmother. So whenever he had any doubts, he looked at the person's nose.

He'd never really spoken to a white person, but he knew all about them because whenever two or more colored people got together, it seemed that the conversation eventually got around to white people. He remembered the evenings at his grandmother's, sitting on the porch with his mother, grandmother, and Uncle Bill, Grandmother's brother. 'You remember William McBell, Fran?' Grandmother would say. His mother's name was Frances. 'That's Isabella's brother, isn't it?' 'That's right.' It would be dark, darker than he'd ever seen anything get. He figured that Pine Bluff must be the darkest place in the world when the sun went down. All you could see were tiny, dark-yellow spots, which were the lights from the coal-oil lamps in the nearby houses. His grandmother lived out in the country, and she said that the white people wouldn't 'run the 'lectric poles out this far, but I wouldn't have none of that stuff running through my house no ways. 'Lectricity put your house on fire. Been using coal-oil lamps for seventy years and got better eyesight than that boy there,' pointing to him. Allen wore glasses.

Grandmother's voice seemed to come from somewhere deep in the darkness, because it was so black on the porch he couldn't see her. There were only those slow voices, the crickets chirping, and the quiet squeaking of Grandmother's rocking chair. 'I believe you went to school with him, didn't you, Fran?' 'He was a year or two ahead of me.' 'Well, they come and got that boy one night.' 'Oh, no!' 'Did. Sho' did. Come and got him and put him on the road gang. That boy hadn't done a thing. He was working every day up here at the mill. He married that McCollough girl.' 'You mean Lucy?' 'That's her. Never can remember that girl's name. Lucy. Well, the high sheriff come and get him one morning. Say he robbed a white man, and they took him off to the county farm up there at Gould and put him on the road gang. These white folks round here do anything and can't nobody do a thing about 'em.' He never said anything, but only listened to them talk about people he'd never known or seen who had come up against that vague whiteness which seemed to hang at the edge of all their lives like storm clouds on the horizon.

It seemed that no one ever had any way of knowing what white people might do, and it also seemed that they could do anything to a Negro and never go to jail for it. That was why he couldn't understand why his father had bought a house in a white neighborhood. There were always stories in the colored newspapers about colored people moving into white neighborhoods and their houses being burned down or the windows being broken or shot out. He hoped that some white kid did come by and try to throw a rock through their window. He'd better have an airplane to get away in, because Allen would catch him and kick his ass. He knew his father didn't mean to let white people burn down their house either.

One day he'd been looking in his father's desk for some writing paper and he came across a gun. It had scared him just to see it, but he put out his hand and touched it lightly. It was cold and heavy and he stared at it for a long time, looking at the long barrel and the round cylinders where the tiny bullets sat. It was strange that those little things could kill a person, but he remembered when Jo-Jo's father had been shot. The police had never caught who did it either. Jo-Jo's daddy had been found early one morning sitting on the curb near the Regal Theater, holding his stomach. He was trying to hold his guts in, somebody'd said. The police took him to the hospital and asked him who did it, but he wouldn't tell. Allen would have. Anybody shoot him better make sure he couldn't talk, because he'd tell the world who'd done it. Tell 'em in a minute. Not Jo-Jo's daddy and for the rest of the year all the kids looked at Jo-Jo with a kind of reverence and awe. 'That's Jo-Jo, man. His daddy got shot.' That made Jo-Jo kinna special. Somebody's daddy or uncle or even mother was always getting stabbed. But that was nothing. Monroe, who was the same age as Allen, had gotten stabbed once himself. He said he was just walking home from the movies one night and this guy hit him on the shoulder and ran on down the street. Monroe didn't think anything about it until he felt an itch in his shoulder and reached up and there was this knife sticking out of it. Monroe said he didn't touch it though. 'If you get stabbed, don't take the knife out. If you do, you'll bleed to death. The knife holds the blood in.' That was good to know, because you never knew when you might get stabbed. Like his daddy always said: 'Niggers are crazy.' Allen carried a knife himself. Everybody did. You got a new knife to go back to school just like you got a new notebook. He'd never used it, though he had pulled it out once on the way home from school. Somebody, he didn't remember who now, had tried to mess with him. He'd pulled out his knife and somebody had hollered, 'Look out, man! Al got his blade! That dude'll cut yo' ass.' Allen was happy that somebody had thought he would use the knife, because he'd been too scared to think what he would do if the guy called his bluff. But, he didn't. 'Aw, Al. I was just kidding. Let's be friends.' The guy had held out his hand, but Allen didn't take it. He'd seen that happen too many times. The guy holds out his hand and you go to shake it and he grabs it and pulls you right into a left cross. Randy had gotten his butt kicked good like that. So Allen simply followed up his advantage and said, 'Uh-huh. Just don't mess with me anymore.' For two days, though, he'd been scared. Just because a dude backed down from a fight on Tuesday didn't mean he wouldn't get his boys together and jump you on Wednesday.

Although the gun frightened Allen, he was glad his father had it. Any white people come to their house, they would be ready. Many times after that he went to the desk when his father wasn't home just to look at the gun. A few times he even picked it up, being careful not to put his hand anywhere near the trigger.

Leroy had almost been killed by Big Time, his older brother, like that. Big Time had been fooling around with his gun and for a joke pointed it at Leroy and pulled the trigger. 'It's empty,' he said as the gun went off. That bullet just missed Leroy's head. Allen always made sure he put the gun back in the same position as he'd found it, and if his father knew he'd picked it up, he never said anything.

Nothing happened when they moved though. Nobody drove by in the middle of the night and shot through the window. They didn't even get any anonymous letters in the mail saying, 'Niggers get out before you're not able.' Allen's father was relieved. 'I told you Nashville was different than other places in the South. It ain't one of them bad towns.' A 'bad town' was one where the white people didn't let the colored live in peace. Memphis, his daddy said, was a bad town. So was any town in Mississippi, Alabama, Georgia, and Louisiana. Whenever he heard those names, he got a little scared. Colored people were still in slavery down there. Once he'd seen the Mississippi River and even it, because of its name, scared him. It was a pretty river too, but why did they have to name it 'Mississippi'?

Allen was a little disappointed that their white neighbors didn't do anything. 'As long as you leave white people alone,' his father had told him, 'they'll generally leave you alone. Most of these niggers who get in trouble asked for it. You just got to know how to handle white people. There's some of 'em you speak back to and some of 'em you don't. But don't never bow your head and act a fool to none of 'em. You hear me? You hold your head up and look 'em in the eye. Say "yes, sir" if you have to. Sometimes that's the only way to get out of certain situations. But don't go saying "sir" if you don't have to.'

And with those words in his ears, Allen went outside to explore his new neighborhood. He hadn't understood most of what his father had said though. He wondered how his father had learned which ones to talk back to and which ones not to. Allen didn't think he would ever learn that. The 'yes, sir' and 'no, sir' part was easy. His father had told him that many times and Allen had learned it so well that he didn't even say 'sir' to his father. He figured that if he could get away without saying 'sir' to his father and not make him angry, white people would be easy.

Rev. Anderson was a medium-sized black man of average build. And he was black! Allen sometimes looked at his father and wondered where the blackness had come from. Even the whites of his eyes were more brown than white. He had come up 'the hard way', as Allen got tired of hearing. Born in Mississippi and raised in Arkansas, he'd worked on a farm with his parents and three brothers. A sister had died while Rev. Anderson was still a boy. His parents died within several months of each other when he was fifteen and Rev. Anderson had had to support his younger brothers. Yet while supporting them on the farm, he'd finished high school, no small accomplishment in 1917 for any Negro, and had gone on to college and from there to seminary. He'd started preaching while he was still a boy – twelve, or thirteen, Allen thought, like his father before him. Allen knew that it was automatically assumed that he would be the third generation of ministers in the family, but it seemed to him that it was time the family tried something new. He wanted to be an artist, a fact he kept carefully hidden. He'd told his father that art was just a hobby, knowing that his father wouldn't let him near any kind of painting materials if he'd thought Allen was serious.

Rev. Anderson had preached in country churches in the South most of his life. He'd met his wife at the little ramshackle church in Pine Bluff. Even now Allen could look at his mother and tell she must've been a knockout when she was a girl. He looked through the family album sometimes and would see pictures of her. She looked white with her pale skin and straight black hair hanging down her back. He wondered why she'd married his father. Everything his father was, his mother wasn't. His father was loud and talkative; Mother was quiet and soft-spoken. Rev. Anderson loved a good joke or story and could tell them for hours. Allen had a hard time remembering the last time he'd heard his mother laugh. And while Rev. Anderson may have gone to college and was a respected preacher, he had little regard for the English language, Allen thought. His father would split a verb, infinitive, or any other part of speech as quick as he would breathe. His mother had very precise speech, and though she'd been raised in the country like his father, you couldn't tell it. Rev. Anderson sounded like he'd never left the country. But Allen had to admit that his father didn't dress like he was from the country. Rev. Anderson always dressed in a dark suit, vest, and tie and he never took them off except to go to bed. Allen had seen his father mow the lawn, rake leaves, clean gutters, and saw wood with his suit, vest, and tie on. And when he finished, there wouldn't be a speck of dirt on him. It was an accomplishment Allen would have liked to emulate if he had been inclined to do any work.

Allen presumed that he looked like a mixture of both of them. He was brown-skinned, and everyone said he looked like his father. But he never believed what people said. They said that for his father to hear. He would have preferred to look like his mother and have hair like hers. He was sorry that he would never know what it felt like to have his hair blow in the wind.

The first few weeks of June were spent getting the new house into shape. Allen had almost perfected a way of getting out of work. Whenever he was asked to do anything, he did as poor a job as possible, angering his mother, who would call him 'trifling and lazy' and finish the job herself. His father, though, would merely say in his deep bass voice, 'Boy, if you don't do it right, I'm going to do some work on your behind.' It was a threat which his father had to give at least once a day while they were unpacking, but Allen knew his father would carry it out. He could recall spankings he'd gotten as a child. His father would go outside and cut some branches from a tree. Though he knew he was about to get a whipping, Allen was always fascinated that his father wouldn't go to just any tree growing in the backyard. He'd pick out certain trees, and through a series of spankings, Allen learned that one kind of tree branch would only burn, while another would sting and make small welts. And another tree would produce a branch that would cut the skin. He could judge the degree of his punishment by the kind of branch his father got, and the day he would never forget was the one his father took branches from every tree in the yard. Great God A-Mighty! He didn't remember what he'd done to deserve that whipping, but he knew he hadn't done it since.

They had moved to a quiet, broad street, where trees with limbs heavy with the green of spring grew from almost everyone's lawn. After he finished working, Allen liked to sit under the big tree in the front yard, though his pleasure was diminished whenever he thought of where those leaves were going to be when October came.

The first few days he felt conspicuous sitting there, but he was also announcing his presence to the world, letting the white people get a good look at him from behind their curtained windows. He did a lot of sketching the first weeks, particularly spending a lot of time drawing the house directly across from theirs. It was a two-story brick house with white pillars and a long sloping lawn. It looked as if it had been patterned after some southern mansion, and in the evenings an old white man came and sat on the porch and stared at them sitting on their porch. 'That ol' cracker's mad as he can be.' Rev. Anderson would chuckle. '"Never thought I'd live to see the day I'd be living with niggers,"' he would say, imitating the nasal drawl of white southerners. '"Niggers getting so they think they as good as a white man."' Allen would laugh too. He liked to hear his father imitate white people, and he too felt proud sitting on the porch. Though their house wasn't two stories, it was made of stone, not common red bricks, and had a sizeable lawn which Allen could take pride in when he wasn't dreading having to cut it. It even had a basement, something their house in Kansas City hadn't had, and his father had built him a room down there where he could go and paint.

But it was obvious that the white people didn't plan to be sitting on their porches long enough for him to do too many paintings of them. All the houses on the block except theirs had *For Sale* signs stuck in the green lawns looking like some man-eating tropical flowers he had read about in science class. He pointed that out to his father, knowing it would be all he needed to continue talking about 'crackers'.

'That just shows how dumb they are,' Rev. Anderson continued on cue. 'One colored family moves on the block and all of them think they got to go. They so stupid. Say we drive down property values. Humph! Much as I paid for this house, ain't no way they gon' tell me a white person would've had to pay that much.' He didn't say how much the house had cost. Money was never discussed, Allen noticed, until he asked for some. 'Just look at those people,' Rev. Anderson went on, stretching out his arm. 'Most of them been living here all their lives, love their homes, but they running to give it all up because of us.' Then he chuckled. 'Boy, we must be some powerful people, you know that? Look at us! We can make a whole block full of white people sell their houses and move. We're something, ain't we?' Allen chuckled with him, but he could feel the hurt and incomprehension in his father's voice. And it didn't make sense to Allen either. What had colored people ever done to white people to make them feel the way they did? As far as he knew, it was white people who'd done to them, but he'd never known a colored person who felt quite so hard about white people the way whites did about them. 'Well, let 'em move. If they ain't got bit no more sense than that, I don't want to live around them. Colored people be glad to come in here and live in these houses. They can't keep us jammed up in shacks all our lives. The Negro's got money nowdays and he wants as good as the next man.'

'This time next year there won't be a white person on this block,' his mother added with concealed delight. It always surprised Allen to hear her speak, but whenever she did, it surprised him even more to hear her agreeing with his father. She was sitting in the swing filing her nails, and Allen hadn't even been sure she was listening.

'That's right,' Rev. Anderson agreed. 'Anybody say anything to you when you been sitting in the yard?' he asked Allen.

Allen was sitting on the top porch step. There were only three, but most evenings when they sat on the porch, that was where he sat. He could've sat in the swing next to his mother, and sometimes he did when he wanted to feel like he was equal to his parents. Other times, though, he wanted to be their son and sat on the steps. 'A few people have spoken when they walked by. Nobody's said anything nasty. They just curious, that's all. Want to know what does my daddy do. And where we're from. I tell 'em and they go on.'

'They just can't get it straight in their heads, I bet,

that a Negro could afford a house in this neighborhood. Only colored people they probably even halfway looked at are maids and cooks and handymen. And that's the only kind they want to see.'

One of the strange things Allen had noticed in Nashville was the old Negro women riding in the back seats of cars driven by white men. At first he'd thought they were being chauffeured, but he knew *that* couldn't be. 'Why those women sit in the back?' he asked his father. 'It looks like the white man is their chauffeur.'

'Well, I guess it does,' his father told him, 'but see, the white man got a problem. If his maid sits up front, then it looks like she's equal to him, like she's a friend. And he can't have that, now, can he?'

Allen still didn't quite understand and feared that white people were more than he would ever be able to comprehend. They seemed to put a lot of time and energy into trying to make black people feel bad.

Their next-door neighbor was a minister who, to Allen, had an exceptionally long nose. Allen saw him every day as he drove in and out of his driveway. He'd been one of those to ask Allen about his family and had volunteered the information that he too was a preacher. Allen had noticed that he had a daughter who looked to be about his age. Now whenever he saw Rev. Van, they spoke politely and the girl smiled but never spoke. It was a nice smile and he was uncomfortable whenever she came out on her porch and he was sitting in the yard.

One afternoon he was sitting out front doing a pen-and-ink sketch of another of the houses on the block. He was getting rather tired of sketching every day, but there was nothing else to do. It was so hot that he didn't feel like trying to meet some of the colored kids who lived a few blocks away. So he sat in the yard and sketched. He didn't know where his mind could've been that he didn't hear her walk up, but he felt something, looked up, and found himself staring at the calves of two very white legs. He quickly averted his eyes, having heard too many times what happened to Negroes who even thought about white women, and it was she.

'I hope I ain't disturbing you,' she said in her nasal drawl.

'Oh, no,' he said nervously, glancing at her for an instant. 'I was just sketching.' He didn't know whether he should stand up or ask her to sit down. But he wouldn't have stood up for a colored girl, so why stand up for her? And he was sure that to invite her to sit down would be a little too friendly, so he looked up at her, hoping that any white person who might see them would just think she was giving him an order of some kind.

'I know. I see you out here every day with your drawing book. I've been kind of curious, so I just thought I'd come over and ask if I could see what you been drawing.'

She was nervous too. Her voice quivered a little and her smile was too eager and friendly. That made Allen feel more relaxed. 'Aw, it's nothing much. I've just been doing different pictures of some of the houses. That's all. It's really nothing.'

'I'd love to see.'

He didn't want to hand her his sketchpad, wishing

she would go away. If she stayed there too long, some of the white people would definitely see them and who knew what would happen after that. She was just trying to be friendly, he knew, but he wondered how many Negroes had been lynched just because some white girl was trying to be friendly. But he handed her his sketchpad.

She looked at each sketch, turning the pages slowly. 'They're really good. That looks just like Mr Riesen's house.'

'Which one is that?' He was curious to know.

'The one right across the street.' Finally she handed the notebook back to him. 'You draw good. Is that what you're going to be when you grow up? Be an artist, I mean?'

'I guess so,' he answered, adding to himself, if I grow up.

'Do you ever draw people?'

'No, I don't,' he lied.

'Oh, I'm sorry. I was hoping you'd do a picture of me.'

He'd figured that was what was on her mind. 'I'm not too good at people. I like buildings better.'

She stood there for a moment more and he knew she was trying to think of something to say, but he wasn't going to help her. A conversation with white people, his daddy had told him, should be limited to answering their questions and in as few words as possible.

'Well,' she said finally, 'my name is Rebecca. Rebecca Van.'

'I'm Allen Anderson.'

'It's been nice meeting you, Allen.'

He didn't reply.

'Bye-bye.'

'Bye.'

He waited until she had walked back to her house before he got up and went inside his. He figured he couldn't sit out front anymore. Not if she was going to make it a habit to come over and look at his sketches, which he was afraid she would. It would've been different if there hadn't been a *For Sale* sign sticking out of her lawn just like all the others. He didn't think he could really be friends with anybody who didn't want to live next door to him.

He was glad his parents had gone shopping. If his father had been at home, Allen knew he would've been in for it. 'White women ain't nothing but trouble,' he'd been told many times. 'There's plenty of colored girls in the world. Ain't no need for no colored boy to be going over in the other race looking for girls.' Allen would sneak a look at his mother and he just couldn't accept that piece of his father's advice. Rev. Anderson hadn't married a white woman, but it seemed to Allen that he'd gotten as close as he could. And once they'd almost gotten in trouble because of it.

They'd stopped at a filling station outside some little town in Arkansas, one summer on their way to Pine Bluff. He must've been ten that summer and was sitting in the back seat, reading. He didn't even hear the filling-station attendant walk up and barely heard his father say, 'Fill it with regular.'

The station attendant didn't say anything for a minute, but Allen sensed that something was wrong and he took his eyes from the book to see a middle-aged white peering into the car at his mother. Finally the man said, 'What you doing with that white woman in your car, boy? You must not be from around here. You one of them New York niggers come down here to show off your white woman? Well, say something, boy.'

Allen was so scared he didn't breathe. He knew his father had a high temper, and he'd heard stories about the fights his father had gotten into with white men who called him 'boy'. So he was surprised when he heard his father say pleasantly, 'And what makes you think she's white, sir?'

Allen knew they were in trouble. His father wouldn't call God 'sir'.

'She looks white to me,' the cracker replied.

Rev. Anderson smiled again. 'I'll admit that she's lighter than a lot of colored people, but now, tell the truth. Wouldn't I have to be a plumb crazy nigger to be driving around with a white woman in my car? Why, if I did something like that, I should be hanged from the tallest tree in the woods. Any nigger with that little sense is too dumb to live.'

The white man chuckled. 'You said a mouthful that time, boy. You didn't look like you was a crazy nigger, but you never can tell. Now, what'd you want? Tankful of ethyl?'

'Yes, sir.'

'Daddy,' Allen blurted. 'You said regular.'

'Shut up!' Rev. Anderson said fiercely. 'Read your book and keep your mouth shut!'

'But –'

'You want me to jerk you out of that seat? I'll

26

take my belt to you, boy, and you won't be able to walk for a month when I finish.'

'Honey,' Allen's mother put in quietly.

'And you keep your mouth out of it too!'

Allen slumped back in the seat, his eyes filling with tears. His father had never spoken to him quite so angrily, and he'd never heard him yell at his mother.

'That's five dollars and forty cents, boy.'

Rev. Anderson paid the man and started the car.

'You be careful, boy. Next time you come down this way, you leave that white-looking gal at home. Some of the white folks down here might not believe she's colored, and I'd hate to think what they'd do to you.' He paused and then added, 'Or her.'

'Thank you, sir,' Rev. Anderson said. 'I'll remember that.'

'You better.' Then he said warmly, 'Have a good trip and drive safe.'

The rest of the trip was made in the worst silence Allen had ever known. Rev. Anderson put the gas pedal to the floor of the car and kept it there.

'Slow down, honey,' his mother said once.

'Didn't I tell you to keep quiet?'

Nothing else was said. From that day on Allen felt his stomach tighten whenever they pulled into a gas station, and maybe he only imagined it, but he thought his father and mother got unnaturally silent too. And whenever his father talked to him about white women, he thought of his mother sitting there in the car, and he couldn't understand why his father had married her if white women were supposed to be bad. Allen knew his mother wasn't really white, but she looked it, even to him sometimes when he didn't think of her as his mother. He wondered if his father ever looked at her that way too. Maybe that was how it was the first time he saw her. He looked at her and he liked her, but he couldn't have her. But then he found out that she really wasn't white and that made his liking her all right.

He didn't know, but it was good his father hadn't been home to see Rebecca standing there talking to him, standing so close that he could have reached out and touched her. He'd never been that close to a white girl before and didn't think he wanted to be again. Girls were complicated enough, and if they were white, he doubted he would ever be able to figure them out. If nothing else, colored girls were simpler.

2

'Got something for you,' Rev. Anderson said one evening.

Allen smiled shyly. His father seldom bought him anything, claiming that he didn't want to 'spoil' him. 'You coming up easy compared to the way I came up. I didn't have no bicycle or anything like that when I was your age. That was unheard of.' Allen never listened when his father started on all the 'advantages' he'd never had. He supposed that he should feel guilty, but it wasn't his fault if he had a bicycle and his father hadn't. Anyway, Allen wasn't even sure there'd been any bicyles back in his father's day.

Rev. Anderson pulled a big sack from his closet and handed it to Allen. He was afraid to open it, afraid that if it was something he didn't like, his disappointment would show on his face. He felt the sack carefully and smiled, because he knew what it was. A basketball hoop! 'Thanks a lot, Daddy!'

'You don't even know what it is.'

'It's a basketball goal.'

'But you don't have a basketball, do you?'

Allen didn't and he knew by his father's tone of voice that he was teasing him. 'That's true,' Allen allowed, going along with the game. 'And without a basketball, a goal ain't much use.'

'I guess it ain't.'

Allen pulled the hoop out of the sack and looked at it, still pretending to be sad. 'It's nice,' he said, feeling the hard metal of the rim. He reached in the sack again and pulled out the knotted strings of the net. 'It's really nice,' he repeated.

'Well, let's go get it up.'

Allen sighed to himself. His father couldn't ever just give him something. He had to make a game of it, tease him a little. Allen wished he'd just say, 'Here,' and let it go at that. Not his father, though.

They went out to the garage, and an hour later the hoop was affixed to a large square piece of plywood and nailed over the garage doors.

'Well,' Rev. Anderson said, taking the ladder back into the garage, 'that looks mighty nice.'

'Sure would be nice if I had a basketball, though.'

'Well, what do you think this is?' his father laughed, coming out of the garage with a ball in his hands.

Rev. Anderson threw the ball to Allen and he bounced it several times. It was a good ball, hard and firm. Allen bounced it a couple of times more, then stopped, jumped, and shot. Two points! His first shot had gone straight through without touching the rim.

'You must think you good!' his father said admiringly.

'I'm pretty good,' Allen returned matter-of-factly.

'Let me see it,' his father said, holding out his hands.

Allen threw the ball to him and his father caught it, dribbled once, and tried a lay-up. The ball hit the edge of the rim and bounded across the yard. Allen ran after it, embarrassed for his father. He threw the ball back to him and his father tried another lay-up and missed again.

'It's been a long time since I had one of these in my hands, you know.' He was breathing heavily as he missed another lay-up.

Allen got the ball as it bounced up the driveway. He dribbled toward the goal, leaped into the air, and shot. The ball made a high arc, hit the backboard, and ricocheted into the basket. Two points! Allen ran down to the basket, grabbed the ball as it came out of the net, and hooked it over his head and into the basket.

'You trying to show your father up?' Rev. Anderson asked, a little hurt in his voice.

'Oh, no,' Allen said, though he thought that maybe that was what he had been trying to do. 'Here.' He passed the ball back to his father.

Eventually Rev. Anderson made a basket and Allen was relieved, hoping that that would be enough to satisfy him.

It wasn't. His father stayed in the yard for another fifteen minutes and eventually he started to make baskets with more regularity. 'I'm getting my eye back now,' he said, making another shot. Allen had to admit that his father wasn't bad, leaping into the air in his suit, vest, and tie.

'O.K.,' his father said finally. 'I'm going to leave it to you.'

'O.K. And thanks a lot, Daddy.'

Rev. Anderson went in the house. Allen sat down on the grass to rest for a few minutes. He hadn't had a basketball goal in Kansas City. The house there had

had a small backyard, most of which his father had dug up to plant turnip greens, collards, spinach, onions, and who knew what else. He liked to farm and sometimes talked about getting a country church again. At one time he'd even raised chickens, but he had to get rid of them because the rooster persisted in attacking Allen anytime he came into the yard. He hadn't been as scared of the rooster as he had pretended though. What he'd really hated was when his father killed a chicken for dinner. He would pick it up by the head and spin it around and around and around, until suddenly the chicken would go flying through the air, blood spurting from its neck. It would jump and hop around, falling over into the dust, kicking and turning until it was dead, the blood dribbling from where its head had been. Allen didn't think there was anything he'd ever hated more than seeing that, but he never talked about it. His father would have laughed at him and called him a girl, as he had when Allen said once that he wanted to learn to play the violin. 'I thought I had me a son. Violins are for girls.' So he'd never gotten a violin and he hadn't said anything about the headless chicken flying through the air. But when the rooster attacked him one morning while he was getting the eggs, he'd pretended to be more hurt and scared than he actually had been. And his mother had eventually prevailed upon the Reverend to get rid of the chickens.

Since they'd moved to Nashville he hadn't heard his father mention anything about a garden and he hoped that he wouldn't have one. The backyard was so big and nice. The garage sat in one corner of it, the paved driveway going between their house and Rebecca's. The yard bordered the lower part of the driveway and extended behind the garage to the alley. A fence separated their yard from Rebecca's and there was also a fence on the other side separating them from whoever lived over there. He wished the fences had been so high that no one could see over. But they were low wooden fences. At least they were there.

He hadn't seen Rebecca for several days, but that was only because he didn't sit in the front of the house anymore. He either stayed in his studio in the basement or sat under the tree in the backyard. He would have preferred to have been in the front, because he liked to watch the people go up and down the street. Too, he wanted the whole world to know that colored people were living there and there was nothing they could do about it. Sitting in the back, he felt like he was hiding himself and he was. But not from the world, just from her.

TWO

I

'DON'T you ever get tired of staying around the house?' his mother asked him one afternoon. He'd just come up from his studio and was passing through the kitchen to go to the bathroom.

'Uh-uh,' he said, wondering why she'd asked.

'A boy your age ought to be out trying to make friends.'

'When school starts, I'll make more friends than I'll know what to do with.'

'Well, it's two months until school starts, you know.'

'I know,' he said. He couldn't admit that he was tired of reading and painting every day. But he didn't make friends easily. Sometimes he wished he had inherited that gift from his father. Rev. Anderson could go anywhere and before the day was out at least half the people in town would know him. Allen didn't appear to be shy, but he was. Particularly around girls. They terrified him. He wondered what other boys said to a girl to get her to be their girl friend. Did they just walk up to the girl and say, 'Will you be my girl friend?' He could never do that, because what if they said no? But what did you talk to girls about? With boys he could talk about girls. Not that he did much talking, but no one ever noticed, because he always laughed loud at the right times and put in enough little comments so that everyone thought he was a part of things even if he didn't feel like it.

In Kansas City they used to gather in the alley in the evening after dinner and sit down with their backs against someone's garage. Somebody, usually Leon, would have stolen a couple of cigarettes from somewhere and they would light one and pass it around.

'Yeah, man,' Leon would start. 'Gloria is nice.' Leon was the same age as Allen, but he appeared to be much older. At least Allen thought so. He was learning how to drive and could take a bicycle apart and put it back together better than anybody. And he knew all about girls. 'And she knows how to use that tongue.'

The other boys laughed and Allen joined them, though he wondered just what Leon meant. Gloria was a cute little girl who lived on the next block, and Leon claimed that she would 'do it' with anybody. All the boys said that, but whatever it was that she would do, she'd never done it with Allen. But he didn't think any girl would. Girls just didn't seem to think of him when they wanted to 'do it'. Maybe that was because he didn't know how to talk to the girls, and Leon said that it was all a matter of 'talking that talk'. Allen didn't like that idea, though. He didn't want to have to convince some girl to 'do it'. If she wanted to 'do it' and he wanted to 'do it', then why did he have to 'talk that talk'? They should just do it.

But girls weren't like that. He'd been in love with a lot, too, and they seemed to expect something from him and he could never figure out what it was. The girl he loved the most was a short girl with sandy

brown hair, which she always wore in braids. She was
light-brown-skinned and reminded him of his mother.
Her name was Ingrid and she played cello in the school
orchestra, and if his father had let him take violin
lessons, he would've been close to her at orchestra
practice. Instead, he sat on the other side of the room
in the clarinet section. Nonetheless, every day after
school he used to walk her home. She knew he liked
her, but she never became his girl friend. It was like
she was waiting for him to say certain things, but he
never knew what they were. He guessed he should've
gone to Leon and asked him what to say, but Leon
would've told everybody about it. 'Allen don't know
how to talk shit!' Eventually Ingrid started leaving
school with Morris. He was one of the dumbest boys
in their class. Allen couldn't understand what she saw
in him. But dumb or not, he knew something Allen
didn't, because Ingrid became his girl friend.

Allen guessed that it would have been a lot simpler
if he hadn't had to worry about eventually 'doing it'.
That was the only reason anybody had a girl friend, it
seemed. But they never said what they did and he was
too ashamed to ask. He knew it was something a man
and a woman did together. He wondered if his mother
and father did it. Probably not. His father was a
preacher and he didn't think preachers were supposed
to 'do it'.

His closest friend in Kansas City had been a girl
named Mary. He couldn't remember when he hadn't
known Mary and she was as close to a real girl friend
as he'd ever had. They used to talk on the phone all the
time, and once Mary had asked him if he wanted to 'do

it' with her. He'd told her yes, but the next time he saw her she didn't mention it. He was glad. Every time they talked on the phone it came up though. One day she'd really scared him when she called and said that her parents were going to be out all day and if he wanted to come over, they could 'do it'. He'd told her that he had work to do around the house.

He'd almost done it one night last summer. They'd all been over at Gloria's house. She had the biggest backyard of anybody in the neighborhood, and some-body suggested they play Hide and Go Get It. It was different from Hide and Seek, because only the girls were supposed to hide. Then the boys would find them. Whichever girl you found was the one you were sup-posed to 'get it' from. Well, he was scared and after all the girls were hidden, he only pretended to be looking. What would he do if he found a girl? And if he found one and she saw that he didn't know what to do, then everybody would know that he didn't know how to 'do it'. He didn't look too hard, but suddenly he heard somebody whisper, 'Allen.'

He pretended not to hear.

'Allen!' The whisper came louder.

It was Gloria!

'Over here by the trash can.'

He didn't have any choice but to go over to her. All around him he could hear girls squealing and giggling and an occasional voice saying, 'Boy, you nasty!' But whoever said it didn't sound like she meant it.

He saw Gloria hiding behind the trash can near the fence by the alley. At least it was dark back there and no one could see them.

'I been wanting to do it with you for a long time, but you act like you don't like me or somethin'.'

'Naw, Gloria,' he protested. 'That ain't true. I like you a lot. I thought you was Leon's girl.'

'Aw, that ol' Leon! He a liar!' Suddenly she yelled, 'You a liar, Leon. You ol' black nigger you!'

'If I'm black,' Leon called back, 'you know what your mamma is!'

'Aaaaaw!' somebody signified.

'You sho' is nasty, Leon,' came somebody else's voice out of the darkness.

'Don't you talk about my mamma!' Gloria yelled into the night. 'At least I got one, nigger. After you was born, your mamma left you in a trash can for the garbage man.'

'Hey, Gloria,' Allen said sharply. Everybody knew that that was true. But even if it was, he didn't think she should have said it. Leon didn't know who his mother or father was. He lived in the orphanage on the other side of town. 'You tell him you're sorry, that you didn't mean it,' Allen implored.

Gloria hesitated, then said a little less loud, 'I'm sorry, Leon. I didn't mean it. We still friends, ain't we?'

No reply came.

'We still friends, Leon?' She was a little anxious now.

'Girl, will you shut up?' came Leon's raucous voice. 'How can I get this good pussy over here if you keep running your mouth?'

Everybody laughed. 'Go 'head on, Leon!'

'Hey, Allen!' he called out. 'Put something in that girl's mouth so she'll shut up!'

'Goddawg,' someone exclaimed.

'Man, that Leon a bad dude, ain't he?'

Allen didn't know what Leon meant, though he had an idea. But he couldn't have meant *that*.

'Allen?' Gloria said softly. 'You gon' do it to me?'

'Uh-huh,' Allen managed to breathe.

'Well, come on.' Gloria took him by the hand, lay down in the grass, and threw her skirt back. He wished now that it wasn't so dark, because he wanted to see 'it'. He couldn't see a thing except her pink drawers and they looked kind of ragged.

'Take your thing out,' she said, pulling her panties down.

He was getting excited now. Finally, he was going to do it. He could hardly wait to tell Leon. He unzipped his pants.

'You got it out?' Gloria asked.

'Uh-huh. You got yours out?' He looked at her and didn't see anything.

'Huh?'

'You got yours out?' he asked again, getting impatient.

'What you talking about, boy?'

Allen felt himself getting warm. Had he said the wrong thing? But he couldn't have. She had to have a 'thing' too, and if she did, she had to get it out. He hadn't said anything wrong.

'You goin' do it or ain't you?'

'Yeah,' he told her again. 'Take yours out!'

'What you mean?' she asked, perplexed.

'Aw girl!' he exclaimed in disgust. 'You don't want to do it. You just playing. I thought you wanted me to

42

do it to you.' He stood and zipped up his pants. 'I ain't got all night.'

'But, Allen –' she began.

'I'm going home,' he continued, sounding disgusted. 'I was sho' 'nuf gon' do it to you, but you just want to play.'

And before she could say another word, he'd gone through the fence gate and was going down the alley toward his house. He was relieved to have gotten out of the situation so easily and only hoped he'd fooled Gloria, that she wouldn't know that he hadn't known how to 'do it' and tell the others. But the next day when he saw Leon and the rest of the boys, all Leon said to him was, 'Man, ain't that Gloria got some good stuff?'

'That's some good pussy,' Allen agreed to an admiring audience, and that had been the end of it.

It was a relief to be in a new city. Maybe by the time he met some kids, he would know what he was supposed to have done with Gloria.

The next morning after breakfast he decided to go walking. What little he had seen of Nashville had been from the back seat of the car when he went downtown with his parents.

'I'm going out exploring,' he told his mother.

'The dishes will be waiting for you in the sink when you get back,' was her only reply.

'Aw, Mamma. I'm the only fourteen-year-old boy in the world with dishpan hands.'

'They'll make a man of you.'

He didn't say anything else. It was good his mother

didn't talk much, because when she did, it was never anything good. She had a smart answer for everything and Allen didn't think she'd ever said a kind word to him in all his life. 'I don't want to spoil you,' was her excuse. There was no danger of that. Even when he showed her a drawing or a painting, she would only stare at it for a minute and then say something on the order of, 'Well, it's all right, I guess, but no artist ever made any money.' Once he'd gotten angry and told her, 'Mamma, it's a good thing you weren't Mary, because if Jesus had come to you and said he was going to preach, you would've said, "You'll make more money if you stay here and help your father in the carpentry shop."' Even before he said it he knew he was in trouble, but if she said what she thought to him, why couldn't he tell her what he thought? It didn't work that way though. His mother reported the remark to his father, who tried to reprimand him. But Allen had seen that little smile at the corner of his father's lips. He probably wished he'd thought of it himself.

Allen paused as he stepped on the porch, looking quickly next door for any sign of Rebecca. No one could be seen at their house and he hurried down the street. It was a hot day, but so was every day in Nashville. He found it hard to believe that the sun was ninety-three million miles away. It felt like it was sitting on top of the telephone wires.

He didn't know if anybody was looking at him from behind their curtains, but he felt conspicuous walking down the street. But then again, he always felt out of place around white people. That is, if he let himself.

44

Whenever he went downtown with his parents, even in Kansas City, he would make himself not see anyone except other colored people. If he could do that, he would be all right. But there were so many white people and it was hard to block out all of them. The only place he'd ever felt really comfortable in Kansas City had been the library. There the white people were outnumbered by books. The library had been next to the Indian cemetery. The Kaw Indians. It was behind a big stone wall next to the library and he used to spend a lot of time there. He had Indian blood. His father's grandmother had been a full-blooded Indian and his mother's grandmother had been half-Cherokee and half-African. She'd married a German Jew and that's why his mother looked like she was white. Allen didn't know anything about Jews except that the Old Testament was all about them, but he was proud of the Indian in him. Not that there was much. When he cut himself while playing and saw the blood trickling out, he would lament silently that it was probably the few drops of Indian blood.

He wondered where the library was in Nashville. They probably didn't allow Negroes to use it, but he wanted to go there anyway. And since he didn't really *know* that they didn't allow Negroes, maybe they did. Or at least he would pretend that they did until he found out better.

He stopped in a phone booth and looked up the address of the library. He'd been downtown enough with his parents to recognize the address. As he walked along the street, the broad green lawns of his neighborhood gradually changed to small patches of grass in front of small houses and he knew that he had entered a colored neighborhood.

'Good morning,' someone spoke as he passed their house.

'Good morning,' he returned. That was something he'd never understood about the South. Colored people spoke to each other all the time. They didn't have to know you. The fact that you were colored was enough. His father enjoyed it, and when they drove down the highway, his father would wave to old people sitting on their porches, kids walking down the highway, men plowing in the fields, and everybody always waved back. His daddy waved at everything colored that wasn't in the cemetery. Not his mother though. She could be friendly when she met someone, but she wasn't outgoing. His father would get into a conversation with a cat if it were black.

'Hello, young man,' a colored man walking past him said.

'Hello, sir.' Allen always made a point to say 'sir' and 'ma'am' to colored people, except his parents.

'How do, son,' said the next person he passed.

'Good morning, ma'am.' He'd be tired just from speaking by the time he got to the library. It was nice, though, people speaking to each other. But he didn't think he'd ever really like it. That was his mother in him, he guessed.

He saw a group of boys playing softball in the middle of the street, but he didn't even pause to watch them. They might ask him to join the game, and he wasn't too good at softball. He could pitch, but when it came to hitting, he struck out every time. Of course, pitchers weren't supposed to be able to hit, but he wondered if that was just an excuse. Maybe he'd become a good pitcher simply because he couldn't hit. Put a basketball in his hand, however, and look out! Basketball was his game. He'd played on the school team in Kansas City, and he guessed he'd remember forever the day he hit twelve points in a game and all from the corner. By the third time he went to the corner, he heard someone yell, 'There goes Al in the corner again!' And he'd jumped and shot a one-hander. *SWISH!* But he was cool. He pretended like he didn't even hear the girls cheering and yelling at him. He just turned and ran back down court, a serious expression on his face, but inside he'd been happy. Once during a time-out he'd looked into the stands and Ingrid had waved at him. But it was just his luck that the next game he was tripped and hurt his knee so badly that he was out for the rest of the season. He still got his school letter, but it was horrible sitting there on the bench hearing the girls yell for somebody else. They didn't care about him. It was the points and they cheered anybody who made points. He wanted a girl to cheer just because it was him. He hadn't decided if he would go out for the basketball team this year. He really liked to play, but he didn't think he wanted to be cheered anymore for making points.

He didn't know how far he walked before he saw a stone building sitting on a hill. That was probably the library. It looked just like the one in Kansas City, gray and ugly. He walked quickly up the steps, studiously ignoring the white faces he passed. He went into the building as if he'd been there many times and walked to

47

the desk. When the old white woman looked up, her jaw dropped. 'What you want?' she said sharply.

'I'd like to apply for a library card,' he said firmly.

'You can't come to this library,' she said nervously.

Allen could feel his heart pounding as he noticed the white people in the library gathering a short distance away. He didn't know what to do, but he knew he couldn't walk out of that library past all those white faces. He couldn't let them run him away. 'Why not?' he said calmly.

'You just can't,' the old woman said, more agitated. She had lowered her head and was busy stamping some cards on her desk.

'I would take proper care of the books.' He spoke distinctly and evenly, betraying no emotion and being very careful not to sound colored, like his father. And though he was angry, his voice was as pleasant as if he were talking about the weather.

'This is the white library!' the old woman blurted out. 'You people have your own library.'

Allen hadn't known there was a colored library, but it didn't matter. 'But one does not have the wide choice of books there that are available here. And I think it's the duty of all Americans to be as fully educated as they can be. Don't you agree?' He almost burst out laughing and wished his father was there to see him.

The old librarian turned a deep red and refused to answer. When Allen realized that she was going to ignore him, he became frightened. He couldn't let her win. He simply couldn't. 'Is there a law against my availing myself of these facilities?'

'Yes,' the woman snapped.

'Might I see it please? I'm not familiar with it.'

'Where you from, boy?' the woman asked evenly, looking at him through narrowed eyes. 'You don't talk like you from Nashville.'

'No, I'm not. I've just moved to the city from Pine Bluff, Arkansas.' And it wasn't a total lie. He had been in Pine Bluff for a week before they came to Nashville. It was obvious, however, that he wasn't going to get a library card. He could sense that a crowd had gathered, and he knew that if he continued to press her something might happen. He didn't know what – she might call the police. But he had to have a library card.

Just then a young white woman came out of a back office. Uh-oh, he thought. The old woman had probably pushed a buzzer under her desk, or somebody went and got this younger one and she was coming out to tell him to leave before she called the cops.

'May I help you?' the woman said pleasantly.

'Yes, I would like to apply for a library card and this woman told me I can't have one. I don't understand why. All I want to do is read.'

'What are you interested in?' the young woman continued.

'Oh,' Allen began eagerly, 'I'd like to see if there's a biography of Winslow Homer. He's one of my favorite painters. And also I'd like the Thayer two-volume biography of Beethoven.' He was sincere, but he was also trying to impress her. She probably thought he was going to list some novels or murder mysteries.

'Well, Mrs Helms,' the younger woman said, 'since I know those books wouldn't be available at the colored library, I don't think we'd be breaking any rules if we let this young man have a card.'

Allen allowed himself to get happy, but the woman had called him 'young man' and not 'boy', and that made him a little wary. No white woman called a Negro anything but 'boy'.

The old librarian was obviously furious, but she only spluttered, 'Whatever you say, Mrs MacIntosh.'

Allen was surprised. The younger librarian was probably in charge of the whole library. The other one probably wasn't even a librarian, but just some ol' white woman who sat there and looked so unpleasant she made people want to read books so they'd forget about her.

'Would you come with me, please?' the younger woman said.

Allen wanted to turn and stick out his tongue at all the white people standing around, but just as he had shown no expression the day he scored twelve points, his face was impassive now. He walked into the woman's office and she handed him a card to fill out.

'These people are funny, aren't they?' she said.

'I beg your pardon?' he replied cautiously.

'I mean their silly rules. They think the library will fall if colored people start using it.'

He didn't say anything, knowing that it was particularly unwise to get into conversations with white people when they were talking against other white people. He filled out the card quickly and handed it back to her.

'You're only fourteen?'

'That's right,' he said pleasantly.

'Aren't you mighty young to be reading such difficult books?'

'I don't think so.'

'Well, we'll have to have your mother or father's permission. Take this card home,' she said, handing him another card, 'and have your mother sign it and bring it back as soon as you can. In the meantime I'll make out a temporary card for you so you can take some books out today. When you bring this other card back with your mother's signature, we'll give you a permanent card.' She sat down at the typewriter and quickly typed out the temporary card. 'I don't know if you know it, but you're the first colored person to use this library.'

'I didn't know.'

'There shouldn't be any trouble though. But this could cost me my job.'

He felt a little guilty.

'I don't think so,' she continued. 'They had me come down here from Ohio to take this job, and I don't think they'll fire me just yet.'

So that was it. She was from the North. He wanted to apologize to her for maybe causing her trouble, but he didn't. He hadn't done anything wrong.

'Let me show you around the library so you'll know where the various books are.'

'Oh, that's all right,' he said quickly. 'I can find everything on my own.'

'It's no trouble.'

Allen glumly followed her out the door. The last thing he wanted was to be shown around the library by a young white woman. It was bad enough that he was there. But the librarian didn't notice his discomfort. The library lobby was empty now, Allen was glad to note, and the old woman didn't even look up as they passed her desk. He hardly listened as the librarian took him through the stacks, showing him what books were shelved where. 'Here's that Thayer you wanted,' she said, bending down and taking two thick volumes from a lower shelf and handing them to him.

'Thank you.' He held the books in his hands for a moment. They were dusty, but he lifted them to his nose and inhaled. There was nothing like the smell of old books.

'Do you like Beethoven?' she asked.

'Yes, but I haven't heard that much,' he admitted. He didn't tell her that his real interest in Beethoven was in the fact that he'd read somewhere that when the composer was a boy he was so dark he was called 'Spangy'. Allen wanted to find out if Beethoven was really colored.

'Ah, and here's a book on Winslow Homer.'

He took the book from her, anxious to get out of there and run home to report his adventure.

'Come with me to the desk and I'll check them out for you. My name is Mrs MacIntosh and if you ever need any help, just ask me. When you bring the card back with your mother's signature, bring that to me.'

'I will and thank you very much.'

He ran practically all the way to his house. Single-handedly he had integrated the Nashville Public Library. That would sure give his father something to brag about. He wasn't even thinking of Rebecca as he passed her house and didn't see her sitting on the porch or hear her run across her lawn to intercept him as he turned up the walk to his house.

'Hi!' she said brightly. 'Where you been hiding?'

He stopped and blinked several times, kicking himself for not going up the alley and coming in through the backyard. 'Oh, nowhere. I've just been busy.'

'You been painting?'

'Uh-huh.' He noticed his father's car sitting in the driveway.

'Can I see what you been doing?'

'They're not too good.'

'Anything you did would be good to me.'

He was anxious to get away from her. 'Well, you don't know much about painting.'

'Maybe not,' she said, visibly hurt by what he'd said. 'But I really did like the one you did of that house.' She pointed to the red-brick mansion-style house across the street. 'Your drawing looked just like it.'

'Thanks.'

'I been watching you play basketball every day too.'

'You have?'

'I can see you good from the kitchen window when I help Mamma with supper. You're good. You don't ever miss, do you?'

He smiled for the first time. 'Oh, sometimes I do,' he allowed.

'Well, I never seen you miss. Can I play with you sometime?'

He didn't know what expression was showing on his face, but he felt like he was three-quarters of the way to being lynched. Everybody on the block was peering out their windows, he thought, and he knew his father was watching. But Rebecca probably didn't notice a thing. He wanted to tell her that she couldn't play with him, that she couldn't even talk with him, but he didn't. What difference did it make anyway if people might be looking at them? They could see he wasn't doing anything except talking. She was just being friendly. He didn't think there was anyone else her age on the block except him. She only wanted somebody to talk to. So what was he afraid of? He had just integrated the whole public library, hadn't he? Why was he so afraid to talk to a white girl? 'I guess so,' he finally replied. 'Just come on over some time when you see me out there.'

'O.K. Maybe I'll see you later then.'

'O.K.'

'Bye, Allen.'

'Bye, Rebecca.'

By the noises from the back of the house he could tell that his parents were eating dinner. His stomach tightened as he walked slowly into the breakfast nook where they ate all their meals. Neither of his parents looked up as he stopped in the doorway. 'I'm home,' he shouted, trying to sound as if nothing had happened.

'We see,' his mother said. 'The food's getting cold.'

'Let me go put these books in my room.' He threw the books on his bed and came back and sat down. His father handed him the bowl of black-eyed peas without saying a word. Allen knew he was in for it. His father was only silent when something was wrong and the more wrong the something was, the quieter his father got. And at that moment, Allen would've thought he was dead if he hadn't kept putting food in his mouth.

'Guess what I did today?'

His parents didn't look up.

'I integrated the Nashville Public Library,' he continued bravely.

'I integrated the library,' he repeated. 'Oh, I have a card for you to sign, Mother, giving me permission to take out books.'

'What were you doing at the white library, boy?' his mother asked, slightly annoyed.

'I checked out some books.'

'They didn't let you do that, did they, Allen?' she asked.

'Those were the books I had in my hand when I came in. They didn't want to let me do it, but they didn't know what else to do with me.' He realized that he was shading the truth slightly, but it didn't matter.

'And 'cause you integrate the library, you think you can come back here and get a white girl friend,' his father interjected.

'Oh, you mean Rebecca?' Allen asked casually.

'So, it's Rebecca, is it?'

'We were just talking. She's not my girl friend.'

'You tell that to her daddy when he comes over here with a rope to get you.'

Allen laughed nervously. 'But she came over to me. She spoke to me first. I was minding my own business. What was I supposed to do? Tell her to go away?'

'In a nice way, yes.'

'But she was only being friendly.'

'Listen, boy. Let me tell you something. Can't

nobody white be friends to nobody colored. You hear me? Friendly, my foot! A rattlesnake be a better friend to you than a white girl.'

Allen knew he shouldn't argue with his father, but he felt like he had when the old librarian had tried to get him to leave. 'I mean, can't two people just talk to each other? Is that a crime?'

'As long as your skin is the color it is, it's a crime. You stay away from that girl. You hear me?'

Allen lowered his head and didn't say anything.

'You hear me?' his father said again, louder this time.

'I hear you,' Allen snapped.

'You watch how you talk to me. You want me to knock you down?'

Allen got up from the table. 'I'm through eating, Mamma.'

'Naw you not!' his father exclaimed. 'Sit down! You leave when I tell you to.'

Allen glared at his father and sat down slowly.

'Now let me tell you a thing or two.'

Please don't, Allen said to himself.

'I'm just trying to tell you something for your own good. You the only son I got and I don't want to see you hanging from the end of a rope. You don't know these white folks. You been up North all your life. But these peckerwoods down here are crazy. You hear me, boy? They crazy! I grew up with a boy named Willie Johnson and they hanged Willie 'cause he didn't say "ma'am" to a white woman. That's right! They took that boy out one night and strung him up. And left him hanging there for a week so all us other niggers could see him. The white man is an animal. He's a beast, and you stay as far away from him as you can. And that means leave his women alone. There're enough pretty colored girls around so that you don't have to go stepping over in the other race looking for a girl friend.'

'We were just talking, Daddy.'

'Just talking! How you think it starts? I know she came over to you first. I was watching. I saw her. But that don't make no difference. There was another boy at home. What was that boy's name? Rufus! Rufus Williams. Rufus was silly enough to be going with a white woman. She wasn't nothing but a piece of white trash, but some of these niggers will take a piece of trash over any colored woman, long as it's white. All of us knew Rufus used to sneak off in the woods and meet her and he'd come back and brag about it. "I got me a white woman" and all kinds of stuff like that. Well, one night he was out in the woods with his ol' white woman and she saw some white men coming. Naturally she got scared, 'cause if they saw her with Rufus they'd lynch her too, so she started screaming and yelling. "Help! Help! Help! Rape! Rape!" And she ran toward the white men just a-screaming and carrying on about this nigger jumped on her. I guess she tore her dress or something to make it look like she'd been attacked. Rufus started running 'cause he knew they wouldn't believe that she was his girl friend. They caught him and killed him dead on the spot. Now everybody around there knew that that girl was no-count. Even the white folks knew that. Wouldn't nobody bother to rape her. It wasn't necessary. But they hung po' Rufus just as high as the rope was long. Now that girl, Rebecca or whatever her name is, might be as nice as they come. But let me tell you, son. She'd do to you what that girl done to Rufus if she was in danger. You might not believe it, but probably right now she's telling her daddy that you started the conversation with her. I know everybody around here done called her daddy to tell him that that nigger boy was talking to his daughter. Probably right now she's saying it was all your fault.'

'She wouldn't do that,' Allen said firmly. And he really didn't think she would. She was too nice.

'Just go on and get up from this table!' his father yelled. 'You sit there and try to defend that pecker-wood to me! Go and get yourself killed! Anybody who's as big a fool as you don't deserve to live. Get!'

Allen left the table quickly and went in his room and closed the door. He fell across his bed, frightened, but glad he had stuck up for Rebecca. His father didn't understand that things were different now. Maybe that was how it was when his father was coming up, but it wasn't like that anymore. Maybe down in Arkansas and back out in the woods it was, but people in the city didn't do things like that. And anyway, he wasn't about to really do anything with Rebecca. He wouldn't have done that in a hundred years. Not because she was white. But she had some kind of funny wire all around her teeth and when she smiled it was like looking into a box of paper clips. He couldn't fall in love with a girl who had wire on her teeth.

Allen didn't come out of his room that evening. When his father was angry, it was best to stay out of the way. Allen wished he could stay in his room for the rest of his life, because when he did come out, it would still be bad. It was the first time he'd ever talked back to his father. They'd had little disagreements before, but never anything like that. He wasn't going to grow up scared of white girls though, like his father. Or of white people. He didn't doubt that what his father had told him about those other boys was true, but that was then. Maybe back then you had to be afraid of white people. He wondered if his father hated white people so much because he was just afraid of them. It reminded Allen of a time in fifth grade. During recess one day Leon and some of the other boys had been talking about girls and they asked him if he had a girl friend. 'I don't like girls,' he'd said coolly. That wasn't true. That was all he thought about, but for a while he'd convinced himself that he really didn't like them. 'I don't need girls,' he used to say. 'They take up too much time, time when I could be painting or reading.' All the other boys respected Allen because he was smart in school, and they were impressed when he said that. But Allen knew he was only afraid of girls. Maybe that was the way his father was. Maybe he stayed away from white people because he was afraid to be with them. If he'd told off that man in the filling station that day, he wouldn't have been afraid the next time he went into a gas station. But now all of them were afraid of gas stations.

He started looking through the books he'd gotten at the library, but after a minute he jumped up quickly and ran to get his dictionary. He leafed through it quickly until he came to the Rs and there he found it.

Rape: 'The crime of forcing a female to submit to sexual intercourse.' He read it over several times, but it still didn't make too much sense. He started to look up *sexual* and *intercourse* but decided to go back and find out if Beethoven had been colored.

2

EVERY Saturday Allen's parents went shopping. Allen usually went too, but this Saturday he decided to stay home. They hadn't been gone long when he went out to the driveway, the basketball under his arm. As he played he was very conscious of every basket he made. He practiced shooting with his left hand and made more than he missed. He wanted to be good with either hand. Although he never looked toward her house, he presumed she was watching. At least she knew he was there. The sound of the ball hitting the backboard and bouncing on the driveway couldn't be ignored, and it wasn't long before he heard a door slam.

He looked around and saw her running across the backyard.

'Hi, Allen!'

'Hi!' he returned, smiling shyly. He looked at her teeth and was surprised to see the metal gone. And for the first time he thought she was pretty. Not as pretty as Ingrid or Gloria, but pretty nonetheless. Her brown hair was cut short and hung down around her ears. Her face was round and she had thin lips. But what fascinated him most were her eyes. He'd noticed them before and sometimes he thought they were brown, but other times they appeared to be green. This morning they looked yellow. He wished that he had eyes that changed colors. His eyes were so dark that one didn't know if they were brown or black. He wasn't sure himself.

'Can I play some ball with you?'

'Sure.'

She climbed over the low fence. 'You're going to beat me, I know. You're so good.'

'I'm not that good. And it's easy when there's nobody playing but you.' He sounded more at ease with her than he really was. He wanted to turn around to see if anyone was looking but stopped himself. If you pretended everything was normal, well, maybe it would be. He threw the ball to her and she bounced it clumsily a couple of times and shot it toward the basket. It hit the rim and bounced away. Allen chased it up the driveway and threw it back to her. 'Take another one.' She bounced the ball and shot again, awkwardly thrusting her arms out and releasing the ball. It bounced off the rim and onto the lawn, hitting the clothesline pole. Allen picked the ball up, dribbled back on the driveway, spun around, jumped, and shot. The ball bounced off the backboard, hit the front of the rim, and richocheted off.

'Seems like I brought you bad luck.'

'Oh, I miss more often than you think,' he conceded.

They took turns shooting for a while and eventually Rebecca made a basket. 'You want to play a game?' she asked.

He looked surprised. 'Sure.'

'I know you're going to beat me.'

'Don't be too sure,' he said, knowing that he was

going to beat her. 'You take it out of bounds first.'
He pointed up the driveway to a drainpipe hanging
down the side of the house. 'That's out. The fence is
out and the grass is out. O.K.?'

'O.K.'

Rebecca bounced the ball clumsily down the driveway. Several times she double dribbled but Allen
didn't say anything. It didn't make any difference
since he knew he could beat her. She slowly made her
way toward the basket, Allen waving his hands in
front of her face. He could have easily stolen the ball
from her but didn't. She stopped dribbling, grabbed
the ball, and drove toward the basket. Instead of
jumping with her to block the shot, Allen moved back
and she scored.

'You just let me do that,' she told him.

He didn't say anything, not sure why he'd let her
do it. He took the ball up the driveway and began
dribbling back toward the basket. Rebecca guarded him
closely, slapping at the ball several times and missing,
but hitting his arm. He maintained control of the ball,
and as he leapt to shoot she pushed him, knocking him
down. His shot didn't go in.

'Hey, that's a foul,' he said, getting up slowly.

'Oh, we ain't playing by the rules, are we? You
know you're lots better than I am. I have to do something to try and even things up, don't I? And anyway,
you're a boy.'

That was true, he thought, so he brushed himself off
as Rebecca took the ball out of bounds. But each time
she went in for a lay-up, which was the only shot she
knew, Allen found himself moving aside and letting

her make it. And every time he had the ball, she pushed him, bumped him, and did anything she could to distract him. He wanted to do the same thing to her, but for some reason he couldn't.

'I won!' she shouted happily. 'I beat you! Let's play another game.'

He shook his head. 'Uh-uh. I don't want to get beat twice in one day.'

'Chicken!' she teased, pushing him playfully. Just then they heard what they thought was a car pulling into her driveway. It was on the other side of her house and they couldn't see it. 'Gotta go, Allen. Maybe I'll see you later.' And before he could reply, she was leaping over the low fence and running across her yard. Just before she went into her house she waved to him. He waved back and had just lowered his hand when he saw her father's car come into view and stop in front of their garage. Allen pretended to be examining his basketball as Rebecca's parents got out of their car.

He wondered if her father had said something to her about him. The way she'd jumped over the fence and run in the house when they heard the car made him think that her father didn't want her talking to him any more than his father wanted him talking to her. Yet she'd come over that morning anyway. She acted like she didn't care what her father thought. And as long as she acted that way, Allen knew he couldn't act any differently. She wasn't afraid of him, so why should he be afraid of her?

Every day he played basketball now and sometimes he saw her getting in the car with her parents or going to empty the trash, but she didn't wave to him. That proved that her parents didn't want her to be his friend. But one morning he saw her parents get in their car and back out of the driveway, and he was sure that they hadn't even gotten to the corner before the back door slammed and there she was, running across the yard, her hair flopping up and down around her face. It was O.K., because his father had already gone to his office at the church where he spent most of each day. His mother was home, though, but he didn't think she would say anything. She didn't seem to be afraid of white people.

'Hi, Allen!'

'Hi, Rebecca!'

'Boy, I thought they'd never go somewhere.'

He tightened when he heard her say 'boy' but decided that she hadn't meant anything.

'My father doesn't want me to play with you,' she continued matter-of-factly.

Allen didn't say anything.

'But he can't tell me what to do. And there aren't any other kids on the block my age anyway.'

When she said that, it made him wonder if she would be playing with him if there were white kids around. He didn't want to think about that.

'I feel kinna funny coming over when they leave. I mean it's the first time I've ever really disobeyed them, and some of those nosy people might tell on me.'

'Well, I don't want to get you in trouble,' he said, wondering why he felt he had to take the blame.

'Oh, I ain't worried. What can he do to me? All he can do is give me a whipping and tell me not to come no more. And the whipping won't hurt long and I'll still come. So, he really can't do nothing.'

Allen had never thought of it that way, and when he did he realized she was right. What could his father do to him? *Really* do to him? Nothing. Absolutely nothing.

'Can I see some of your paintings?'

'Sure,' he said.

She climbed over the fence.

'I'll go get them.'

'Can I come?'

'It'll only take me a minute.' Part of him wanted her to see the studio his father had built and his big drawing board, just like the ones at school. But he really would get in trouble if anyone saw her going into his house. He wanted her to see how neat and clean he kept the room too. He kept his sketchpads and watercolor paper on one shelf. On another were empty jars, his brushes, and the watercolor paint tubes. On the walls he put his favorite paintings, not only those he'd done, but copies of paintings by Winslow Homer and Edward Hopper. He guessed Hopper was his favorite. He liked the way everybody and everything seemed frozen in Hopper's paintings. And he had a feeling that maybe that was the way things really were. Things only appeared to be moving or changing, but really they weren't. Like the people he used to watch working in the cotton fields near his grandmother's. All day long he'd watch them, and although he knew they moved up and down the rows with their hoes, they looked the same. And every day it was like that. And every year when he went back they were there. Maybe they were different people, but it didn't matter. It was the same.

Nobody ever saw his paintings except his mother, and he didn't know why he continued to show them to her. She never seemed to like any of them. Maybe if he had a good art teacher in school that fall, he would show them to him. But he felt his paintings were the real him and nobody had ever known the real him. The thought of somebody doing so frightened him. He took her a series of still lifes he'd been working on. He liked vases and jars and glasses. They were hard to paint, but there was something about glass that excited him. Cloth too. He always painted his still lifes against a cloth background, which meant he had to paint not only the glass, but the cloth as it looked through the glass. It was very difficult, but he was proud that he'd been able to learn to do it fairly well. Or so he thought at least.

He walked through the kitchen, where his mother was peeling potatoes. 'I'm going to show Rebecca some of my paintings,' he said pointedly.

'You'd better hope your father doesn't find out.'

He smiled to himself. That meant she wasn't going to tell him, but if his father did find out, she wouldn't defend him. And that was O.K. with him. Just as long as she didn't tell him.

'Here're a few,' he said, handing the paintings to Rebecca.

'Wow!' she exclaimed. 'They're really good.' She sat down on the grass and spread the three paintings in front of her. 'That's a pretty vase.'

'It's my mother's.'

'And that coal-oil lamp!'

'Oh, I did that at my grandmother's. She doesn't have electricity, and there're all these coal-oil lamps all over the house.'

'I haven't seen one of those in a long time. When Daddy was preaching down in Eufaula, Alabama, we lived in a house that had coal-oil lamps. We put in electricity, though, and only used the lamps for a little while. I never realized they were so pretty till now.'

Allen smiled.

'You paint some funny things.'

'What do you mean?'

'This one,' she said pointing to the last painting. 'I would never have thought to paint a picture of some old mason jar.'

He laughed. 'I like them. They're thick and – and well, I don't know. I just like them.'

'I wish I was an artist.'

'Oh, you can be. Just get yourself some paints.'

'It'd be a waste of money.' She handed the paintings back to him. 'I don't have any talent for anything. I can't even sew. I'm a horrible cook, my mother says, and just plain good for nothing.'

'I bet you could do anything you really wanted to.'

'But there's nothing I want to do.'

He'd never met anyone who didn't want to do anything. 'Oh, I bet there's something.'

'Well, there is one thing,' she said, starting to smile.

'What's that?'

'Play basketball with you!'

She laughed, but he could only manage a weak grin.

'O.K.,' he said glumly. 'Let me take these back in the house. The basketball is inside the garage.'

When he came back out, she was practicing her lay-up shot. He took a few practice shots, hitting each one. He was determined that she wasn't going to beat him today. She took the ball out first. He moved in to guard her. 'No fair,' she said. 'You're bigger than I am, and play better. You shouldn't guard me so closely.'

'But you beat me. Remember?'

'Luck. That's all that was. Luck.'

He backed away, still determined that every time she drove in for her lay-up, he would block it. When she did, though, he dropped his hands and watched the ball go up, touch the backboard lightly, and drop into the basket.

He took the ball and came down the driveway, dribbling rapidly. She slapped at his arms, squealing excitedly. He dribbled the ball between his legs to get it away from her, but she stayed right with him. She pushed him softly, but he maintained control of the ball and began to drive toward the basket. She shoved him, placing her hands against his chest, and he lost the ball. She laughed as she ran and picked it up and ran toward the basket without dribbling and made her lay-up. 'Four to nothing, my favor.'

By the time the game was over he was angry. She had scratched him once, pushed him constantly, and he wanted to hit her in the mouth. But not only didn't he hit her, he couldn't even bring himself to try and steal the ball from her, afraid that he would miss the ball and touch her hand. So she beat him again.

'What's wrong, Allen?' she teased after the next game. 'Am I too good for you?'

'I guess so,' he agreed. He wondered if she really thought she was better than he was. She knew how well he could shoot.

'Well, I'd better be going,' she said. 'My folks will probably be back any minute. And thanks for showing me your paintings. Do you ever go out sketching?'

'Sometimes, but not since we moved here.'

'You should go over to Peabody College.'

'Where's that?'

'Just a few blocks from here,' she said, pointing west. 'There's the prettiest building over there I've ever seen. It has a lot of big columns or pillars or whatever you call them. Down home we call 'em posts.' She laughed. 'It sits way back and there's all this pretty green grass in front of it. It's almost like a park. I've always wanted to go over there and just lie in the grass.'

'Maybe I'll go over there one day.'

'Could I come?' she asked eagerly.

'Sure. I guess so,' he said, frightened as he heard the words come from his mouth.

'Let's go Monday.'

'Uh – O.K.'

'Tell you what. I'll meet you at the corner of 18th and Horton at, say, one o'clock. We can walk over from there. It's only a couple of blocks.'

'O.K.' He was glad to see that she wasn't dumb enough to ask him to meet her on her front porch.

'Bye, Allen.'

'Bye, Rebecca.'

The minute she left his stomach started hurting. It always did when he was really scared, and when he thought about walking down the street with her on Monday, his stomach felt like it was trying to grind rocks and glass. He should have told her no, but he couldn't. And it was silly to be scared anyway. All they would be doing was walking down the street. That wasn't a crime, was it? He wouldn't hold hands with her or anything like that. But he knew that that wouldn't make any difference to anyone. He couldn't back out though. Not if she didn't, and he didn't think she would.

He stayed in his studio all that evening, a piece of watercolor paper tacked to his drawing board. But he didn't paint, though he had his tubes of paint, a jar of water, brushes, and a plate of glass on which to mix colors on the small end table next to him. He drew a rough sketch of a tree on the paper, but his mind wasn't on it.

'What's the matter with you?' his father asked when he came upstairs.

'Who, me? Nothing.'

'Wrestling is on TV tonight.'

'I think I'll go in my room and read.' He left the parents sitting in the living room looking at television. His mother didn't watch it much, but he and his father did every night. They'd been the first ones on their block in Kansas City to get a television, and he had been so fascinated by it that when he came home from school, he'd turn it on and sit and watch the test pattern. He didn't care what was on. Sometimes he'd sit and watch the white lines on the screen when even the test pattern wasn't on. So if he wasn't watching television, he knew his father knew something was wrong. Rev. Anderson probably thought he was still upset by their argument at dinner the other day. At least Allen hoped that's what he thought. His mother probably knew it had something to do with Rebecca, though she didn't know he was going out with her Monday.

Allen left the house about twelve thirty Monday afternoon. Maybe Rebecca had forgotten and wouldn't come. Or maybe she had something else to do. When he got to the corner where they were supposed to meet, she wasn't there, and he sat down on a stone wall and waited for her, a sketchpad and pencils in his hand. He'd brought all of his pencils, because he did intend to sketch. He didn't know whether or not he'd complete it though, never having seen the building. But he'd brought all of his pencils, even the ones he used for dark shading.

He saw her when she was two blocks away. She had on a green dress, and in the midst of his fright he felt a twinge of joy. It was the first time he'd ever really gone someplace with a girl. She started running when she saw him and was out of breath by the time she got to him.

'Hi, Allen!'

'Hi, Rebecca!'

They started walking. Allen was very aware of the people staring at them from the cars that went by. Some people actually turned around in their seats, as if they couldn't believe what their eyes told them they were seeing. Others slowed down ominously to get a good look at them. But nobody stopped. Allen tried to eradicate them from his mind, like he usually did when he was around white people. He wondered if Rebecca noticed the people. She didn't seem to.

'How did you come to start drawing and painting?' she asked.

'I don't know. It's just something I've always done. I guess it must've started in school and the teacher said it was good, so I did another one and that one was good too, and I did another one and here I am.'

'Is that what you want to be when you grow up? An artist?'

He shrugged, thinking she'd asked him that once before. 'Artists really don't make much money, so I don't know.'

'That doesn't matter, does it?'

'You can't live without money.'

'Oh, sometimes I think people make money too important. That's why I don't know what I want to do when I grow up. What I'd really like to do more than anything else in the world is just travel. Just go everywhere in the world and see all the different kinds of things there are to see. That's really what I want to do. But I probably won't, because you need money. That ain't fair, is it?'

He shook his head. 'But that's the way it is.'

'That's just what my daddy says. "That's the way it is." Do you ever get tired of "the way it is"?'

He wondered if she really knew what she was asking him, or if it was just a question to her like any other question. The first thing he'd thought of was white people and how they were always doing things to Negroes. He thought about the filling station and the people driving by staring at them that she didn't seem to notice. He thought about how much his stomach hurt and how he hoped nothing would happen to him because he was going to spend the afternoon with her. 'Yes, I do,' he said somberly. And he wanted to tell her all of those things and to talk about his father and hers, but he didn't. Maybe it was just a question to her.

'You could be an art teacher,' she said.

'No!' he almost shouted. 'I don't want to be a teacher.'

'Why not?' she asked, a little taken aback.

'I just don't. If you're going to be an artist, be an artist. Or if you're going to be a teacher, be a teacher. But don't be a teacher because you can't be an artist.'

'I never thought of it quite that way. Do you think a lot?'

'I guess so. I don't know.'

'I do. I think all the time, but I didn't know anybody else did. Would you believe that you're the first colored person I ever talked to?'

'Oh,' was all he could manage.

'If my daddy could see your paintings and know how smart you are, I bet he would like you. I bet if he really knew you were different than other colored people, it would be all right.'

He didn't know if he was supposed to be glad that he was 'different'. He supposed he was. She had meant it as a compliment, but it didn't make him feel good.

'There it is!' she suddenly exclaimed.

He looked and saw a building sitting several blocks away at the end of the college campus. He'd never seen so much grass in one place before, and the building at the far end of the lawn looked like an ancient Greek temple with its columns and the dome on top. 'How do we get closer to it?' he wanted to know.

'Let's just walk across the grass. I really don't know. This is the first time I've been over here. I've seen it a lot when we've driven by and I always wanted to come and lie on this grass.'

They walked up a driveway and went across the grass. They were still some distance from the building when Allen stopped. He wished he could find a tree they could sit under where they wouldn't look so conspicuous, but there was none in the center of the lawn and this was the best place from which to sketch the building. He sat down on the grass and opened his sketchpad. He looked around, relieved that they couldn't be seen from the street.

She sat down beside him. 'Do you mind if I talk while you draw?'

He shook his head.

'Isn't it pretty here?'

He nodded.

'Every time we go by it in the car I say, this is where I want to go to college. Are you going to college?'

He nodded.

'Well you could come here too,' she said, getting excited. 'Wouldn't that be fun?'

He didn't nod this time. She thought he was like her, he guessed. She didn't seem to know that he couldn't go where she went. In fact, every place she could go, he couldn't. But she didn't know that and he didn't want to tell her. If he did, he was afraid that she'd just feel sorry for him.

He took a hard lead pencil and began sketching the main outlines of the building rapidly. She started to say something else, but he cut her off with, 'I guess you can't talk. I'm sorry.' But that wasn't it. He always listened to the radio when he painted and it never bothered him. He just didn't want to hear her anymore. She would talk about all the things she wanted to do or did do, and all of them would be things he couldn't do. So he didn't want to hear her. She made him feel, sometimes, like he didn't exist.

She sat beside him quietly and he could feel her eyes looking at his sketch and at the building. Once he turned to her and noticed her pale arms. The top of her dress was curved, and once when she leaned over to look at the drawing, he inadvertently looked down her dress. All he saw was her brassiere, white and stiff, and the pale white skin of her shoulders, but it was enough to make him turn away as if he'd been slapped. She was sitting so close that their legs touched slightly and he wanted to ask her to move a little. He could have told her that she was disturbing his concentration. But that wasn't it. He was just afraid again and because he was, he didn't ask her to move.

After sketching in the main outlines of the building with a hard lead pencil, he retraced it in a pencil with softer lead, making the lines more definite, and began indicating the shadows on the columns, roof, and beneath the portico. One day he would get closer to the building and do it in detail. He could tell that there were intricate designs on the building, but right now all he wanted to do was to put it down as he was seeing it for the first time.

He became less and less aware of her as he worked and was a little irritated when he felt her tapping him on the shoulder. 'Huh?'

'Do you know that colored man?' she asked, pointing to an old man in work clothes who was beckoning to Allen from the edge of the grass.

Allen didn't know anyone in Nashville and wondered what the man wanted with him. Had somebody seen them and was going to call the police? 'No, I don't know him.'

'He looks like he wants to talk to you.'

Allen got up and walked over to the man. 'You want me?' he said belligerently.

'Son, you ain't from round here, is you?'

Allen shook his head.

'That's what I told 'em.'

Allen felt like a thief who'd been caught.

'They told me to come out here and talk to you. If you didn't know no better, it was one thing, they said. If you did, it was another.'

'What're you talking about?' Allen said brusquely.

'The white folks around here at the college been looking at you sitting out there with that white girl. And they don't like it, son.'

'They don't have to,' Allen shot back.

'They don't like it one bit,' the old man continued, as if he hadn't heard. 'Some of 'em wanted to call the po-lice, but I told 'em I'd come out here and talk to you. I told 'em they didn't need to be calling no po-lice.

77

You looked like a nice boy who didn't want no kind of trouble or nothing. Now, son, maybe where you come from it was all right to lay around in public with white girls. But the folks down here don't like that and I just thought I'd tell you. I'd hate to see one of my people get in a whole mess of trouble just because they didn't know they was doing something they shouldn't be doing.'

'You through?'

'I done said my piece, son. It don't matter none to me who you with. To tell the truth, I'm glad you with one of theirs. They do anything to our women they wants to. That's my feeling about it. But you know how it is. I sho' wouldn't like to see them call the po-lice on you. Not if there was something I could do first.'

Allen was suddenly ashamed of the way he'd talked to the old man. He nodded his head and muttered softly, 'Thank you. Thanks a lot, sir.'

'Don't mention it, son. Us colored folks got to stick together.'

Allen walked slowly back toward Rebecca, his head lowered. His face was burning, and he was glad he wasn't white because he would have turned as red as blood. He didn't say anything but reached down and picked up his sketchpad and pencils.

'Do we have to go?'

He nodded. 'He said we couldn't sit on the grass.'

'Well, just for that, I'm not going to come here to college. I'll go someplace else. This is the prettiest grass in the world too.' She got up and they started to walk away.

'Listen,' he began. 'I have to go somewhere, so maybe I'll see you later.'

'Can't I come?'

No, silly white girl, he told her silently. 'No, I have to run an errand for my father.'

'O.K. I sure had fun, Allen. Maybe we can go somewhere else sometime where they'll let us sit on the grass.'

'Yeah. Maybe so.'

'Well, bye, Allen.'

'Bye, Rebecca.'

He didn't have anywhere else to go, but he didn't want to walk back with her. He couldn't go through that again. Every car that passed might have somebody in it who would do more than stare. He walked in the opposite direction from the one she took and just kept walking. It had been a stupid thing to do. He'd known that all along. Well, maybe she might want to go someplace again, but he wouldn't. Once was enough. He couldn't understand why she was so eager to be with him. What did she want from him? She didn't know anything about him, because if she had, she would've known that they couldn't really go out of his backyard. But she could get him into a lot of trouble if he let her. All he needed was for her to invite him to her house one day and to be there when her folks came home. Or to let somebody see her coming out of his house when his parents weren't home. There was no place for them except under the basketball net.

It was late afternoon when he walked up the alley and came through the back gate to his house. He had a feeling that she might be sitting on her front porch waiting for him. He didn't want to see her. He wasn't even sure that he ever wanted to see her again.

Allen walked in the back door and through the kitchen. 'I'm back,' he said glumly to his mother, who was standing at the stove.

'Don't go anywhere. Your father wants to see you.'

'About what?'

'You know what.'

Allen didn't know how they could've found out so soon. 'Where is he?'

'He's taking a nap. He'll be up in a little while and will want to see you first thing.'

He went into his room and waited uneasily for the sound of his father's footsteps in the hall. He was afraid to even imagine what his father would do to him. He jumped when he heard the knock on his door. 'Come in,' he said nervously.

His father came into the room slowly. 'You busy?'

'No, sir,' Allen said. His father didn't look angry, but Allen decided he'd use a few 'sirs' for good measure. They couldn't hurt anything.

'I had a visitor today.'

'Who?' Allen asked, trying to sound no more than normally curious.

'Rebecca's father.'

'What did he want?'

'He claimed that somebody called him and said they saw Rebecca walking down the street with a colored boy. And he figured it was you. Was it?'

Allen started to lie but changed his mind. He was sure his father knew the truth. 'Yes, sir.'

'I told him it couldn't have been, but I figured it was.'

'We went over to Peabody College and she watched me while I sketched a building. That's all.' Allen opened his sketchbook so his father could see the drawing.

'Didn't I tell you to stay away from that girl?' his father asked, but still not showing any anger.

'Yes, sir.'

'But you got a mind of your own. Is that it?' His voice remained even and Allen had never known him to be serious in this way.

'I don't know, Daddy. I know what you said and all that, but – but, I can't explain. It was just something I had to do.'

'No matter what might happen to you.'

'I just couldn't be afraid of a white girl. That's all.'

Rev. Anderson nodded, as if he understood. 'Well, her father was fit to be tied. He was yelling and carrying on about "Keep your boy away from my daughter or I'll have him put in the penitentiary." I told him if he tried that he'd better be prepared to go meet St Peter, 'cause I'd kill him dead.'

Allen's eyes widened.

'Well, he kinna calmed down when I said that. These peckerwoods are cowards. That's why you ain't never heard of just *one* of 'em coming to lynch a nigger. They got to get thirty or forty together. I told him that my son was a good boy and as far as I was concerned his daughter was lucky that you'd even talked to her, because you didn't talk to just anybody.' Rev. Anderson chuckled. 'Well, he didn't know what to say to that. He come over here expecting to scare the daylights out of me, and when I stood up to him he had to back down. I told him you were a good Christian and he didn't have a thing to worry about. I laid it on thick and he calmed down. He didn't like it one bit, of course, but I don't think he'll cause any trouble.'

Allen didn't know what to say.

'You just be careful. Don't get in a position where anybody can even think you might've been doing something wrong with her. You understand?'

'Yes, sir.'

'Long as people can see what you doing, you'll be O.K., I guess .'

Allen couldn't believe that his father had changed his mind. It was too good to be true.

'Anyway, he said that he believes they've found a buyer for the house, and if everything goes through they'll be moving out by the first of September.'

The news hit Allen harder than he would have imagined. He had stopped thinking that one day she might move. But that was probably why his father wasn't too upset. Rebecca would be leaving and that would solve everything. Still, Allen was pleased that his father had defended him. He could've acted like he had with the man in the filling station.

'Well, you better go wash up. I think your mother's about got supper ready.'

3

ONE evening about a week later when his father came home, he said, 'Well, I guess your girl friend is getting ready to pack. I didn't see the sign out front this morning.'

And the three weeks before she moved went by so fast it seemed hardly longer than a day. Now that they didn't have to hide, he and Rebecca saw each other every day. She was knocking on his back door the first thing every morning. Mostly they played basketball and Allen resigned himself to never winning a game. But he came to enjoy her pushing and bumping him. Her hands felt warm against his chest when she pushed him and it made his body tingle. But as much as he wanted to, he could never make his hands touch the bare arms that were inches away. He wanted to maneuver himself so that his hands could 'accidentally' brush against her chest, but he couldn't make himself do it. He used to feel all over Gloria when they played, but Rebecca wasn't Gloria. If Gloria had gotten mad when he touched her, which she never did, he could've hit her. But if Rebecca got mad, he didn't know what he would do. So she beat him game after game, day after day. Twenty to two. Twenty to four. Twenty to nothing. He told himself that this was a good chance to perfect his long shot, and sometimes he would shoot from as far back as the drainpipe and once or twice he got lucky and it went in. That was like shooting from mid-court. He would take quick, hasty shots before she could bump into him or push him. And some of them went in. But when the game was over, it was always Rebecca the winner.

Once she suggested that they go for a walk, but he said, 'Let's stay here. It's better here.' And she hadn't argued. Everything was all right as long as her parents could see her, he figured, and he made sure that they could.

Whenever they weren't playing basketball, they lay on the grass and talked. He showed her his art books and felt sad when she didn't like Hopper's paintings.

'Everybody looks like they're dead. Or they look like the dummies you see in store windows. People don't look like that.'

'Yes they do,' he insisted. 'It just depends on how you look at 'em.'

'Is that the way you look at me?'

'Sometimes,' he admitted.

'Well, don't,' she said getting angry. 'I don't want you looking at me like I'm dead. I ain't dead!'

'I know that, Rebecca.' She'd once told him that he could call her Becky, but he preferred Rebecca. She wanted to call him Al, but he told her no. Allen was his name.

She liked Winslow Homer a little better, but not much. 'You're the only artist in the whole world that I like,' she told him one hot afternoon.

He laughed. 'I'm the only artist in the whole world you even know.'

'That ain't got nothin' to do with it,' she insisted. 'But you paint things I know about, like coal-oil lamps and mason jars.'

He wanted to tell her that he was planning a surprise for her, but he didn't. Every evening, though, he worked on two paintings. One was of the building at the college. He'd gone back several times and made more sketches, but he liked the one he'd done on the day they went, with the building sitting in the distance, and in front of it, the best grass in the whole world. The grass was harder to paint than the building, because he wanted it to look so good to her that she would think she could lie in it. And in the winter-time he wanted her to look at the picture and lie on the grass and forget about the cold snow on the ground outside. The other picture was of her. Every day he studied her face until he was able to draw it from memory from almost any angle. And finally he'd decided to paint her face-forward, with her hair hanging down about her cheeks. His favorite of the dresses she wore was the green one with the curved top. It made her eyes appear green too. Every night he worked slowly and carefully, making sure not to make her look like she was dead. When he finished, he knew that it was the best work he'd ever done. He almost didn't want to give the paintings to her. But he'd done them for her and it wouldn't be fair to keep them. They were really hers anyway. And maybe when she looked at them, sometimes she would think of him. That was what he really hoped.

Near the end of August she stopped coming over as much. They had begun to pack and she would sneak away when she could and they would stand at the fence and talk until a voice came out of the basement of her house yelling, 'Becky! Becky! You better get on back in here and get to packing these dishes.'

Allen never left the yard though. He played basketball, imagining that she was there playing with him. He brought the ball down the driveway, dribbling low and fast. He spun around her, and before she could regain her blance he drove toward the basket and made an easy lay-up. Two points! She came down the driveway, bouncing the ball. Easily he slapped it away from her and dribbled down to the basket and made another quick lay-up. Her ball again. He let her dribble toward the basket and she went up for a shot. He went up at the same time and their bodies collided, but his hand went out and slapped the ball as it left her hand. The ball skittered over to the fence. He ran, picked it up, and without moving, made two from the corner. Six to nothing. Every time she went up for a shot, he was there, his body banging into hers as he blocked her shots. And he won. Twenty to two. He'd let her make one so she wouldn't feel bad.

After supper she had more time, but they couldn't stay in the back of the house. It was dark back there and he remembered what his father had told him. So they would sit on his porch step. His parents would stay in the house, but the door was open and he knew they could hear every word through the screen. But he didn't mind. At least her parents knew where she was and they were in full view of anybody who wanted to see.

'I really hate to leave,' she said one night.

'I wish you didn't have to.'

'I tried to convince Daddy that we shouldn't sell the house. But he said that he didn't want to live around colored people. I told him that you weren't colored. I mean, you are, but you're nice.'

Allen hoped she talked about something else, because if she kept on, he was so afraid he wasn't going to like her. And he didn't want to do that.

'He just said we had to move. Will you come visit me sometime?'

'You'll have your own friends when you move. You won't want to see me.'

'That ain't true. I don't care how many friends I have, I'll always be glad to see you. You're the nicest boy I ever knew. And that's the truth.'

'And you're the nicest girl I ever knew,' he felt obligated to say. And maybe it was true. He didn't know.

'So will you come see me?'

'If you want me to. You call me up some time and I'll see if I can get my daddy to bring me to your house.'

'O.K. And you better come, too.'

'I will,' he promised, but he was certain that he wouldn't. 'You be sure and call me. Even if I can't come out, we can talk on the telephone.'

'And you can tell me what you're painting.'

He gave her the paintings the night before she left. She couldn't see them well in the dark and ran over to her house to look at them. When she came back, Allen thought she had tears in her eyes. 'They're beautiful! They're really beautiful! And they're for me?'

He nodded.

'That grass looks so real I want to lie down in it.'

He smiled. 'That's what I hoped you'd feel.'

'Allen?'

'Huh?'

'Am I really that pretty? Am I? I never had nobody do a picture of me before.'

'I think you are. I painted you just like I see you.'

'I'm going to put both of them up on the wall in my room, and when you get famous I'll tell all my friends that I knew you when you were a kid. Of course, you will have forgotten all about me by then. You'll be living in New York or Paris or one of those places and wouldn't even remember me.'

'That's not true. And you know it,' he said firmly. He would never forget her.

'I was only teasing,' she said softly.

He wanted to kiss her good-bye, but they only shook hands awkwardly when it was time for her to go. 'We're leaving pretty early in the morning, so I probably won't see you. I'll call you. O.K.?'

'O.K.'

'Bye, Allen.'

'Bye, Rebecca.'

The next morning there was no one at the house next door except the moving men. By noon they drove away in their big van and a little while later another moving van stopped in front of the house. Some Negroes got out of a car, a man and a woman and two little children. Allen went to the backyard and played basketball so he wouldn't see them move in.

She never called and he hadn't thought she would, but the first few days after she moved, he rushed to the phone each time it rang. One day his father saw him moping around the house and asked, 'You miss your girl friend?' He said it gruffly, but Allen could hear a little concern in his voice too.

'I miss Rebecca.'

'Well, don't let it get you down. She probably has some white friends now and has forgot all about you. You'll meet some nice colored girl at school.'

He did. Eloise was in his art class and she had to be the prettiest girl he'd ever seen in his whole life. She wore her hair in two pigtails and was dark-skinned like his father. She had big brown eyes and always dressed nice. Allen didn't know what to say to her, but this time he was determined that he wasn't going to sit back and let somebody else make her their girl friend. He started making little sketches in class and passing them to her. He still didn't know how to 'talk that talk', but he could draw. Maybe that was just as good. He drew a little sketch of her. She didn't say anything, but when he saw her put it in her notebook, he knew that she'd liked it. The next day he did a sketch of himself walking her home, and after school she was standing outside waiting for him. And that had been it. He hadn't said a word, but she was his girl friend.

Her mother and father worked, so there was never anybody home when he walked her from school. At first they would sit outside and talk, but one day she invited him in. Immediately when they were alone, he wondered if she wanted him to 'do it'. He was still too afraid to even kiss her, so they drank Cokes and talked.

But one day it happened. They were sitting on the couch holding hands and before he knew it Eloise was kissing him so hard that she cut his lip. After that they practically ran to her house every afternoon. He never 'did it' to her though. She was afraid she would have a baby and he was just plain afraid. But they did everything else. He even saw 'it' and 'it' didn't look anything like he'd thought. No wonder Gloria hadn't taken hers out. He wished he could've told Leon about Eloise.

He hadn't thought about Rebecca for months when he saw her one Saturday during the Christmas vacation. He'd gone shopping with his parents and while his mother was in one store, he and his father decided to go to another store just to browse. They were going up on the escalator when he saw that head in front of him. He knew immediately it was her. As much as he'd studied that head! As many sketches as he'd torn up before he'd finally gotten it right! There couldn't be another head in the world like it. Her back was to him, but it was her. He knew it was.

'Rebecca!'

Practically everybody turned around except the head he was shouting to.

'Rebecca!'

He watched her get off the escalator, and now he could see her clearly. It was her! She was with another white girl. 'Rebecca!' he shouted again and she turned, looked directly at him, and turned back around.

He stopped, not knowing what to think. Maybe she really hadn't seen him and he pushed through the crowd. He was almost on her now. 'Rebecca!

Rebecca!' He put out his hand to grab her by the shoulder when he felt a hand on his other arm. He turned around and it was his father. Rev. Anderson's grip on Allen's arm was gentle but definite, and Allen looked into his father's eyes. He was afraid he was going to cry and he knew his father could see that. The two stood there for a moment and Allen was suddenly aware of all the white people staring at him. He continued staring at his father, and when Rev. Anderson looked away, Allen knew that his father had recognized her too. It *was* her and she *had* heard him. His face felt warm all over like it had the day the old colored man told him to leave.

Without a word he and his father found the down escalator. When he got home, he asked his father for a screwdriver. 'I want to take down the basketball goal.'

'You giving up basketball?' his mother asked. 'What's the matter?'

'I'll give you a hand,' his father interjected quickly, ignoring her question.

'Thanks, Daddy.'

Allen held the ladder while his father took a crowbar and pried the backboard loose from the garage. He handed it down to Allen. 'You want to give it to some poor kid at church, Daddy?'

'What do you want to do with it?'

Allen thought for a minute. 'I guess I should give it to somebody who could use it, but – but I really would like to throw it, throw it – ' And unable to hold them back any longer, he cried.

His father put his arms around him and hugged him

tightly. He didn't say anything and Allen was glad. He didn't want to hear any stories or any advice. He just wanted to cry.

And he did.

By the same author

LONG JOURNEY HOME

Here are six rich and haunting tales woven from the bare threads of historical fact. These stories are of ordinary men and women, not great figures of history: there is the one of runaway Louis and his escape on the 'underground railway'; Bob the black cowboy who knew the ways of the wild horses and could skilfully steal a herd from its stallion; Rambler the lonely blues singer who, no matter what the temptations, could never bring himself to stay in one place; Jake and Mandy, forced apart when she was sold with their children.

Beautifully crafted, these proud, painful, glowing stories capture the very essence of black history.

TO BE A SLAVE

The first blacks arrived in America in 1619, and it was nearly 300 years before slavery was finally ended by the Civil War in 1865. This book is based on the memories of former slaves who recall their inhuman treatment at the hands of white owners. It is the harrowing and remarkable story of a people who endured terrible hardships while maintaining a fierce sense of worth and pride.

Runner-up for the Newbery Medal, and winner of the Lewis Carroll Shelf Award and the Nancy Block Award.

THE FIRST OF MIDNIGHT
Marjorie Darke

To eighteenth-century Bristol where the slave trade continues to flourish in defiance of the law, and from the shores of Africa, comes Midnight bearing a sense of his own humanity which triumphs over the evil scheming slave masters. Befriended by Jess, herself a slave, Midnight battles for his freedom.

LET THE CIRCLE BE UNBROKEN
Mildred D. Taylor

The story of the Logan family's attempt to lead a decent life in racist Mississippi in the 1930s. A long, sophisticated book but one which offers great rewards.

MARTINI-ON-THE-ROCKS
Susan Gregory

Eight short stories about teenage life in a multi-racial urban setting. From battles with teachers to a young Hindu wedding, to the problems of being with the in-crowd: an extremely absorbing and contemporary collection.

THE DISAPPEARANCE
Rosa Guy

A powerful story about a young boy on probation who tries to make a success out of living with his new wealthy foster family.

EDITH JACKSON
Rosa Guy

The story of a young black orphan, struggling against poverty and prejudice to keep together the remnants of her family. (Sequel to *The Friends*.)

GANESH
Malcolm J. Bosse

Jeffrey has lived in India and America, but where does he belong? The fascinating story of a young boy growing up and finding his way in two different places.